BREAKING INTO
THE SAFE OF LIFE

S
U
S
A
N

C
H
E
R
R
Y

CHICAGO SPECTRUM PRESS
LOUISVILLE, KENTUCKY 40207

CHICAGO SPECTRUM PRESS
4824 BROWNSBORO CENTER
LOUISVILLE, KENTUCKY 40207
502-899-1919

Printed in the U.S.A.

10 9 8 7 6 5 4 3 2 1

ISBN: 1-58374-075-9

SOMETIMES, "I" IS I;
SOMETIMES, IT'S A LIE.

CONTENTS

COMBINATIONS

CROWBARS

TREASURE

COMBINATIONS

SIX SURREAL MINUTES

This chamber
where I'm strapped
to my seat
begins to dim
as if afflicted
with cataracts.
Medusa, dressed
in snowy lace,
sashays across
a stage of glass,
her tresses
hissing lustily
until they're swiftly
swept away
by fingers
large and flaccid
as lasagna
laid to dry
upon Goliath's
pasta rack.
They sweat
with effort
as they slap
whatever comes
across their path,
then transform
to twirling skirts
that vanish
in a sudden gust,
leaving behind
a residue
of diamond dust.
I lurch into light,
relieved my car
is finally clean.

COGNITIVE DISSONANCE

I came of age in the Age of Protest

when red, white, and blue
were the colors of blood
and absence of reason and deep despair

when fifty thousand invaded the nation's
sacred city of monuments,
their fingers forming the letter "V"

when stars and stripes were torn and torched
and the cast of *Hair* despaired in song,
I'm falling through a hole in the flag.

Breathing the rage that blew like a gale
through my wide-open youth,
I grew to disdain

the *America—love it or leave it* refrain,
which grimaced the faces of those I admired
like a rock song performed on a harpsichord.

Now I stand in a crush of candles and flags,
singing an anthem whose words wax and wane
in my memory like classmates' names

and as I sway with compatriots
who mourn the attacks on the nation they hated
so passionately

past and present grind together
like bones that have lost their cartilage,
creating a scraping I can't ignore.

A JOURNEY THROUGH THE DAY

Dawn showers in snores
laces up her shoes of dew
and puts on makeup

*

Wrapped in newspaper
commuters drink their coffee
from cups of scramble

*

Climbing up the hours
the sun stops at the summit
to eat a sandwich

*

Unfinished business
hangs onto our sleeves and hems
like a clingy child

*

Seduced by the stove
taste buds strip and spread their legs
hoping for climax

*

Determined fireflies
dot every "i" of twilight
in neon yellow

Darkness *do si do*s
with the daughter of fatigue
to slumber's fiddle

THE MUSIC OF DOUBT

The hands
          of ambivalence
scurry about
          the keyboard
of the heart,
          siblings who vie
for Decision's ear
          as they execute
repeating themes
          in different keys
from a score
          without rests
or double bars.

READING "THE GREATS"

Love it's not,
even though it's supposed to be.

The poems arrive in tails and cummerbunds,
roses in their white-gloved hands,

and escort me to five-star establishments,
where every waiter knows them by name.

They never spill wine on their ruffled shirts,
never say "was" instead of "were."

They lead as we waltz, frowning slightly
whenever I step on their patent pumps.

I endure their caresses, pretending their fingers
aren't cold and rubbery as whales,

and silently crave a polka, a beer,
a peppery tryst in a Chevy's back seat.

OPERA IN THE PARK

As the city becomes a pointillist painting
of white on a background of deepening black,
thousands of people on picnic blankets
wait for the diva to take them away
from the horns and the heat and ubiquitous hawkers
who thicken the August smog with insistence.

The prima donna sashays on the stage
in elbow-length gloves and a red satin gown,
her naked shoulders adorned with a boa
of sequins reflecting the light of her verve.
Her Mozart infuses the twilight with sparks
that ascend to the heavens and turn into stars

while just blocks from this flash of magnificence,
a homeless man plunders an over-filled dumpster,
a runaway teenager needles his arm,
a robber holds hostage a family of four,
a gang member pummels a rival to death.

SELECTIVE RETENTION

We yearn
for our turquoise
college days,
forgetting
the pressures
that piled up
like a pyramid
of gymnasts.

We hunger
for the years
our children
fluttered about
on silver wings,
forgetting
the tantrums
in check-out lines
and crayon embedded
in the rug.

We dress
our resurrected dead
in golden robes,
forgetting
the flaws
we cursed before
the earth embraced
their pale flesh.

The paint box
of Time
contains no black
or gray or beige.

PANTHEON

This temple of symmetric perfection,
built two thousand years ago
to please capricious deities

sits in the middle of modern Rome,
its sixteen columns grounding a city
that flies as fast as Jupiter's bolts.

Behind its triangular pediment
and hulking doors of ancient bronze,
sunlight cascades through an open dome,
as if ladled from an Olympian bowl.

On the plaza outside,
where the fearful once placed
their sacrifices to the gods,
the hopeful now hawk an array of goods:

rubber rabbits that hop when squeezed,
key chains with plastic Pietas and Davids,
silver-sequined halter tops—

the daily mating
of sacrilege
and the press to survive.

FIRST CLARINET LESSON

This bafflement of wood and steel
lies dismembered in its case
like music phrases unarranged.

I grease the corks and join the pieces,
handling each as if it were
as fragile as my confidence,

then suck the reed, remembering
the wooden licks that finished off
the popsickles of childhood.

I stiffen up my lips and blow,
hoping for a healthy G,
producing not even a kitten's squeak.

Hoarding air, I try again,
this time siring a shriek
I fear will summon the police.

I start to crave my piano days,
when even the tentative touch of a key
created tonality stainless as prayer.

Repositioning my tongue,
I blow until my cheeks transpose
themselves into a minor key.

My fingers, rounded on the holes,
gradually begin to sag
like ledger lines below the staff.

My teacher gives a helpful tip,
says she'll see me in a week.
I swab the spit from my instrument

and slink out to my minivan,
where the radio smirks a medley
of Benny Goodman's greatest hits.

LEVIATHAN

The past swims
in a holding tank
like a whale who aches
for the open sea
but cannot flee
the blue concrete,

a creature who feeds
on raw remembrance
tossed from stinking pails.

We stroke its clammy
tail and fins
to earn its trust, learn
to ride upon its back,

and ponder how to set it free.

TWO KINDS OF SILENCE

One
steers the car
as you drive your child
to school each day,
rubs your feet
as you read by the fire
while your spouse
plays Solitaire,
wafts your hair
on twilight strolls
with a friend you've known
for twenty years.

The other
spills the coffee
as you breakfast
with your teenager
who tiptoed in an hour late,
extinguishes the candles
when your date professes
love you don't feel,
flings the valises
when guests announce
they plan to stay
another week.

Two kinds of silence,
identical twins
with temperaments as different
as the dream
from which you wake awash
in tranquillity
and that which terminates
in tears.

ON A DOWNTOWN STREET

There he goes again, telling another kid
I'll get sick if she shares her cookie with me.
If the shoe were on the other hoof,
there'd be sugary treats every hour of the day
for circling this pasture of steel and glass
like a mindless mare on a merry-go-round.

Does he really think these flaps on my bridle
keep me from noticing buses and cabs
that assault my nose with their halitosis
and pummel my eardrums with hisses and beeps?

How would he feel if instead of that tux,
he had to parade through the months attired
in valentine hearts and bunny ears,
American flags and witches' hats, not to mention
blinking lights attached to his receding locks?

Oh, for the years when I ran the trifecta,
kicking up dust like a Kansas twister,
thousands of devotees shouting my name,
certain I'd win them a lakefront estate,
a Lincoln or Lexus, an emerald necklace.
Now they expect nothing more than a snort,
a toss of the head, a flash of the teeth
in my dollar-a-minute, seven-block trot.

The latest clan clambers into the buggy
to snuggle under a red, plaid blanket.
I brace myself for a tug on the reins
that will catapult me into the traffic,
wondering how Pegasus learned to fly.

WASTED ENERGY

Good intentions
huddle in your nucleus,
befuddled by a painful past
that orbits them frenetically,
engendering a negative charge
excuses cannot neutralize.

Locked away for decades
in the lab of obligation,
I try and try to extricate
a single circling particle,
hoping to reverse the charge,
to make what once repelled attract.

Yet even with the best of tools,
success is as invisible
as atoms to the naked eye.

I throw away my microscope
and focus on the seeable.

DAISIES

Every Friday for forty years,
Papa came home from his job in town
with an overwhelm of yellow daisies
neatly wrapped in cellophane.

He'd present them to Mama as if he'd just
corralled a galaxy of suns.
She always acted surprised as an ingenue
given her very first bouquet.

Carefully, she'd cut the stems
and place them in the same, blue vase,
while Papa glowed like a supernova.

Once, when she was polishing
a table under the newest blooms,
she suddenly confided

that she'd hated daisies all her life.
"But don't tell Papa," she exhorted,
swearing me to secrecy.

Today I place a modest bunch
of irises upon her grave
beside the lavish, yellow spray
Papa will replace next week.

MOTHER-DAUGHTER GETAWAY

Weeks before you shed the skin
of dependency, we drive

to a place where leisure's flute
charms the snakes of daily life.

Zipping past acres of planted
land, we stuff ourselves

with chips and chatter,
batting wisecracks back and forth

like shuttlecocks, dissecting
the past and present with laughs.

And as the very best of us
pours out until it inundates

the irritations and injuries
that propagate in family blood,

I wonder if this weekend trip
will give us strength to say good-bye

or make it that much harder
when you ride into tomorrow's smile.

PARADOX

The refrain
of the rationalist
blasts in my brain
whenever a newscast
reports on the latest

fatal crash
or bombing raid,
shooting, looting,
mugging, rape,
epidemic, famine, flood,
mud slide, quake, or hurricane:

There is no God.
There is no God.

But when my spouse
is hours late,
my child's fever
just won't break,
or waiting for my test results
sets serenity aflame,

the singing
of the thinking mind
transforms into entreaty
to a Being whose existence
I'll continue to deny.

TAE KWON DO CLASS

Shoeless students in tunics and sashes
bow to their master, a child-sized giant
who left his smile in Seoul.

Transforming into contortionists,
they fracture boards with naked hands
and kick the air like January.

You roar and grimace with the group,
you who've been placid as drizzle in June
for all the decades we've been friends,

and I wonder why I never knew
that thunder and lightning
were sparring behind your tranquil eyes.

BALM

Relentless
as the sun
of Greece,
obligation
beets and blisters
the sensitive skin
of serenity
until it flakes
like baklava.

I slather myself
with the aloe
of art
to soothe
the pain and itch.

RETURN TO ROMANCE

Freed from the cell of celibacy
by this first undoing of a snap,
I panic like a prisoner
who aches to once more taste the world
but can't remember how to swallow.

The warden in my head commands
I cuff your hands before they start
to peel my baggy uniform,
which skillfully conceals the puckered
flesh that rides my thighs and hips,
the purple varicosities,
the breasts that tiny lips have made
balloons from last week's birthday bash.

I cling to you like a child who fears
abandonment for inadequate grades
and pray your eagerness for me
will not be jailed by middle age.

MISSING THE YOU I KNEW

The day always sang as we strolled the campus,
propelling each other with our minds.

You were my idol, so different from me
with your probing ways and uncanny knack

for mapping my past without being there.
You taught me to look

at the world through prisms
instead of panes,

to unwrap the maxims
that came with my packages from home.

When we'd put our diplomas in golden frames,
we married our sweethearts

and settled down on opposite coasts,
barraging each other

with letters about the soul of the world
and the world of our souls

until Motherhood rewrote you
in an alphabet I didn't know.

I studied it but couldn't remember
the dozens of puzzling characters.

Our missives transformed into breezy notes,
then fizzled out like unfed fires.

I think of you now when I least expect—
in the boardroom or on an Aegean cruise—

and wonder if in future years,
when your children are taking campus strolls,

you'll still remember how to bend
exclamation points into question marks.

GOD'S LITTLE ODDITIES

Coconut

Punk-haired teenager
hard-headed as December
sweet as May at heart

Ginger

Kali of the ground
burning buds with the torches
in her many arms

Artichoke

Green-collared canine
whose intimidating bark
is worse than its bite

Kiwi

Pudgy scatterbrain
always misplacing razors
needing a clean shave

Cauliflower

Herculean fist
blistered from its macho vow
to avoid sunscreen

Onion

Modest ingenue
aggressive under layers
of thin petticoats

MATERNAL INSTINCTS

My toddler floods the noonday calm,
a bubbling concoction of babble and squeal,
gripping and releasing my hand
as she stops to bat the shafts of sun

when suddenly, a screech of feathers
blitzkriegs from a sequestered nest,
grazing the pate of my hatless tot,
reddening her towhead tufts.

I thrash the air like a branch in a storm,
scoop up my child and bolt for home
as the winged attacker swoops again
and snares my hair like a crochet hook.

Cursing the bird, I stumble inside,
wash the wound and soothe the cries,
astounded when the thought occurs
that the creature and I are two of a kind.

WUNDERKIND

"Proceed along the path that you have hitherto trodden so
splendidly and so gloriously. Nature and art vie in making
you one of the greatest artists."

*—Ludwig van Beethoven in a 1794 note to
14-year-old Franz Clement, a child prodigy violinist*

Dazzling the masters with matchless technique
and an ear as keen as puberty's stings,

you started to conquer the concert halls
when your peers were still playing hide and seek—

a Mozart who, without a score,
transcribed complete orchestral works

and once amazed an audience
by playing the violin upside down.

Ah, Franz, the envy of all you'd meet,
why don't we know your name today?

PARENTS' WEEKEND

The tower inks its spire with sun
and autographs October's sky
as if to say *Remember me?*

as if I could forget the days
we cursed its tone-deaf bells from tattered
couches in your student suite, where we sipped
instant coffee and laughed about classes
you'd skip each time I visited
this white-and-crimson paradise.

The bells still clang as middle-aged,
I walk the crunchy campus paths,
barely able to keep pace
with him who could have been your clone
two decades and a half ago,
long before we placed the wreath
of ivory roses on your grave.

He introduces me to friends
he's known for only several weeks—
his family now, he says, and I
remember how your mother wept
the day you made the same remark.

He takes me to the dining hall,
where students load their trays with extra
fruit they'll sneak up to their rooms,
as if they had been taught by you.

Whoever thought, a year ago,
when you and I drank pink champagne
to celebrate the letter
from this place where opportunity

grows thick and green as ivy
on the omnipresent brick

that being here with him today
would be so very bittersweet?

AMERICA, 2001

Nature's gallery teems with creations
Autumn, manic as Van Gogh,
produced in several sleepless weeks.

Yet no one sees the masterworks
of orange and yellow, red and brown—
only a solitary canvas
Fear has painted black and gray,

still wet as tears,
without a frame.

OPTIMISM

pops out
of the loam
of youth,
a dandelion
woven from golden
shafts of sun.

It brashly butters
the field of being,
thumbing its nose
at those who dare
to call it a weed,
till storms and heat
bleach and thin
its pluckiness,

which mounts
the whimsy of the wind
and rides into
another life,
leaving behind
a feeble spine
on a bristle of leaves.

CROWBARS

ANGER

Beneath the impossible
child-proof cap,
the impervious foil
and wadded cotton,
potent tablets
wait to heal
the pain
that silence
births and feeds.

I store them
in a cool, dark place
and watch the bottle
gather dust,
too afraid
of side effects
or overdose
to break the seal.

INSOMNIA

Brawny thoughts in tees and shorts
stretch each night beside my bed,
then jog around my spouse's snores,
sweating lists of this and that.

I hear them pant as they unclog
the tunnels running from their hearts,
lifting weights of the day just past,
chinning themselves on tomorrow's bars.

At dawn, they'll dress in suits and ties
and bustle off to work refreshed,
while I ignite my lifeless flesh
with pots and pots of hot caffeine.

MOTIVE UNKNOWN

Planted in a mound of grass
at the public park

is a plaque engraved,
Fluffy, our beloved friend.

The creature beneath is a mystery,
maybe a poodle or Persian cat.

In purple marker Nature's brushes
will never be able to scrub away

a teenager scrawls a four-letter word
on the epitaph.

Perhaps he will win a particle
of popularity with friends

or siphon off a drop of rage
he doesn't know is in his veins

or transform for awhile
into more than a pawn

on the checkered board
of adolescence.

He saunters to the snack bar
while across the sea

a museum encases The David in glass
to prevent another blow to the toe

and a welder mends The Little Mermaid's
severed head.

STRESS

ascends the ladder
Life constructed
from the bones
of Chance
and picks our apples,
tossing them
in bushel baskets
on the grass,
totally indifferent
to preventing
slashes in the skin
or bruises
in the juicy flesh.

Limbered
from this warm-up
like a pianist
who has practiced scales,
it strips our leaves
and stitches them
together in a quilt of green
it brashly steals
for itself,
then gnaws our trunks
with beaver teeth
it sharpened
on our impotence.

We tumble to the ground
in halves
and wait for insects
to invade.

TRYING TO CONCEIVE

It's always worst in springtime,
when the heavy coats that have long eclipsed
the waxing moons of the mothers-to-be
move into other orbits, revealing glories
that glow in the light of growing life.

Omnipresent as oxygen, the full-wombed
flaunt fecundity in grocery stores,
balancing like gymnasts as they reach
for milk and melons, in ticket lines,
where one takes up the space of two,
and on the bus, with briefcases
that slide down their laps like leather sleds.

Months from now, they'll push their strollers
in the sun, suckle in their rocking chairs,
inhale the scent of promise
as they bathe and powder perfect flesh

while their neighbors are having frantic sex,
plotting the most propitious time
for egg and sperm to unify,
only to curse the determined blood
that stains their relationship month after month

and produces an ache far worse than the pain
of childbirth.

SELF-PITY

The scent
of solace
lures us
through a door
that bolts
behind our heels.
The keyhole
closes over
like a shutter drawn
against the cold.
We amble
through a labyrinth
where light begins
to dissipate
like reasoning
at sleep's approach.
Candled by our neediness,
we stumble on, oblivious
to the rumblings
of the Minotaur
who waits for us
within the core.

SURPRISE!

You were the best favor
in the grab bag,
the sparkly ribbon
wound this way and that,
forming a sphere
of treasures
that presented themselves
when I least expected,
like flowers delivered
one at a time
from a secret admirer.

I delighted
as each prize appeared,
stashed the treats
in the massive pockets
of my wonderment,
until a crasher
halted the party
abruptly as the tune cuts off
in Musical Chairs.

I had to uncoil
the remaining twine
at home, alone,
discovering as I neared the core
not tiny books and cars and rings,
but rusty nails and razor blades.

I cleaned and bandaged
my bleeding hands,
knowing I'd never have the heart
to reveal my find
to those who shared
my gleefulness
when I'd unreeled
the layers easiest to see.

OBSESSION

is a giant dune
that changes shape with every gust

showering grit on daily life
like rice upon a bride and groom.

It plugs the ears and floods the eyes,
peppers tongues and open wounds

piles up in socks and shoes
until it hampers every move

growing fast despite attempts
to bulldoze it with intellect.

CAMPUS VIGIL

Solemn as an altar boy,
he stands alone
in a dense confluence
of estrogen, a candle
in his mittened hand,
and listens to tales
black as the night
he supposedly owns,
though he doesn't remember
taking possession.

A girlwoman shakes
as she tells how rape
has washed away
concentration and sleep
like a giant wave
that leaves behind
a smattering
of empty shells.
Another speaks of flashbacks
that throw punches
when she's off her guard,
knocking her out
in a ropeless ring.

The stories spill
with frenzied speed.
They penetrate
the youth's green parka,
freeze upon his reddening cheeks,

while the man in the moon
listens with a frigid face,
then disappears behind a cloud,
darkening a campus path
where a coed screams.

REJECTION

Sometimes we hear
the murmur
of its wheels
a mile
down the track,
though we cannot see
its brassy beam
or feel vibrations
under our feet.

Other times it suddenly
engulfs us
like a giant wave
from a motorboat
we paid no heed
as we floated
sunblind
on our raft.

Either way,
rejection plucks
the engine
from our confidence
and sells it shamelessly
for scrap.

SHOPPING FOR COLLEGE

With six weeks left before you go,
we poke through aisles of merchandise,
scrutinizing towels for flaws,
examining lamps and drying racks,
as if the wrong choice could hex your success.

You gleam as I pile the wheeled cart
with blankets and sheets, a bulletin board,
a radio, a sewing kit, a clock with an alarm that chirps,
as if cramming the basket's every cranny
could fill the hollows in my heart.

I load our purchases on the conveyor,
faking excitement, trying to cover
the anguish of losing what never was mine—
the child I birthed, then relinquished to time.

PERPETUAL CYCLE

Defying prediction, your nimbus clouds
burst like piñatas on my garden

and in an instant, weeds spring up
to overtake the radiant blooms
I've worked so hard to cultivate.

I spray the invaders with rationalizations
to which they're immune,
dig up their roots with worn-out tools
forged in the fire of woundedness,

too focused on the task at hand
to notice that on the way to the trash,

the interlopers drop new seeds.

THE UNRESOLVED

nips and barks
like a terrier,
digging holes
in flower beds,
peeing on fences
erected from scraps
of complacency.

Lock it in a cage
of distraction
and hide the key
in denial's vault,
but it will escape,

determined to gnaw
the meaty bones
of days long gone
and chase serenity
into the street.

SEXPECTATION

Millions of females

full-term fetuses curled together
in secrecy's womb,
waiting and waiting to be delivered
into the light

pickled in blood
and unable to move,
yet unaware of the others' presence,
sharing the guilt and resentment
the placenta sends through tired cords
that coil around their necks like snakes

Millions of females

unwanted offspring of Obligation
who dream of escape
with the cut of a blade

REAGAN SUCCUMBS TO ALZHEIMER'S

Long ago
I hated you
for vaporizing
all I prized
on the burner
of your say-so.
But when I read
of your diagnosis,
my enmity
transmogrified
to empathy,
a Hyde-turned-Jekyll
in seconds flat.

I envision the lab
inside your head,
a clutter of beakers,
dishes, and tubes
that shatter
without warning,
spewing their contents
on memory's floor,
where they mingle
into lethal concoctions
that seep into reason
and acumen,

dooming you
to be a leader
history will not forget,
yet one who'll die unable
to remember being
President.

GUILT

You bring it on yourself—
or not—

like choosing to drink from another's glass
or being forced to sit beside
a sneezing person on a bus.

But no matter how the germ
is passed—

sometimes, like a basketball,
sometimes, like a classroom note—

it packs your gut with icicles
and turns your slumber into slush,
reproducing ceaselessly,
for spreading is its destiny.

POTENT POTION

Every morning, the blade of impatience
grinds a scoop of wishfulness

I dump in the unbleached filter
of fate. I fill my carafe with water cold

as a corpse's kiss. Blackness drips
and steams like a geyser about to erupt.

I pour the brew in a bottomless cup,
drink it with copious sugar and cream,

hoping it won't burn my tongue
or permanently stain my teeth

before it slings me into the day
with a slightly bitter aftertaste.

SEIZURE

Dancers storm the ballroom
and without so much
as a warm-up waltz,
begin a tarantella
to the tambourines and castanets
of Chance's band.

Their restless feet accelerate with every bar
until the hall begins to shake like a Richter Scale 8.3,
shattering panes of window glass, flinging paintings
from their frames.
Sweat cascades like lemonade
poured by a child who can't control
the pitcher's lip; breath becomes a gymnast
on a trampoline

until Exhaustion
shuffles in with broom and pan,
flicks off the lights

and starts to sweep
debris where it

cannot be seen.

REIGN OF TERROR

Robed in foreboding, Cancer
overtakes the throne
and lifts a scepter of despotism
destined to ravage
his realm.

In whispers,
he orders sporadic forays
on hamlets of his new domain,

while the populace pulls the window shades,
pretending all is well despite

occasional cries that loiter like cats
at a garbage dump.

The raids begin to escalate, and panic
infiltrates in tanks
that trample
the taken-for-granted.

The natives stockpile rationalizations
that good behavior in the past
will keep them safe.

But many flee without bothering to pack,

while Cancer surveys the chaos
with glee, flabbergasted
at the ease

of bringing complacency
to its knees.

WAITING FOR THE TEST RESULTS

After the vermilion vials
have been lined up in their plastic trays
like soldiers at inspection time
and the Band-Aid
has been ripped from the skin,
leaving its fingerprints behind,
and the deep deep breath
has been held and released
held and released
and the peek-a-boo gown
has shed its leaden pinafore
and all that's left of the cherry shake
is a coat of radioactive paint
on the walls of a giant plastic cup
and the padded conveyor
has ventured in and out of the tube
like a child at play in a sewer pipe

the patient goes home
and totes the phone
as if it were an oxygen tank
while she scrubs the basement,
irons her socks, rearranges
her knickknacks and photos

and wonders which will be deadlier—
the diagnosis or the wait.

DOCTOR EXPLAINS
THE BRAIN SCAN

Their bellies facing skyward
on the banks
of a fluorescent pond,
twenty turtles
sunbathe
in my sizzling gaze,

indifferent
as they're prodded
by the pressed white coat
who tries to coax
the future
from their spotted shells
but can't do more
than change the rays
I shine on them

to sudden rain.

OPERATION

We got it all
the surgeon says,
beaming like a child
who has scooped
his jack-o-lantern clean.

He vanishes
into a scramble of scrubs
and gloves and masks,
never to be seen again
except as a scrawl
on a stack of prescriptions.

I lie on starch, melting
like the citrus sherbet
on my tray.
Nurses and aides
with identical smiles
prod me
with gauges and instruments
like meteorologists
tracking down storms.

Soon they'll give away
my room,
successful at stopping
my oozes and throbs
but not the ambiguity
infusing my future
like IV fluid.

PROGNOSIS

The graph line
plummets
like a chute
to the Underworld,
predicting my future
in fractions.
The doctor
interprets, furtively
checking his watch
to ensure
we don't exceed
our ten-minute limit.

His words bounce off
my brain
like baseballs
pitched too fast.
I ask the same questions
again and again,
like a child
who pleads
till he gets the answer
he wants to hear.

I picture my body
displayed on satin,
catching tears
like a weathered basin,
my molded mouth
no longer able
to ask *Why me?*

I beg for reassurance
that my illness
isn't hiding
in my offspring
like a robber
but receive
no guarantees.

As another patient
invades the room,
I return to a world
where roses still open
and friends still chat
over cups of tea.

CARE-GIVER

kaleidoscope of emotion
rotating in the hands
of Chance

solitary icicle
melting and re-forming
as the mercury rises and falls

mechanical pencil
filling in blanks
with a breakable tip

cratered planet
obscured by the supernova
of cancer

AWAITING CHEMO

Dolly dangling from her hand,
the child scampers back and forth
between the lab and pharmacy,
oblivious of those who watch
from chairs with wheels locked in place
like baby buggies at the park.

A skeleton ensconced in sweats
reaches out to touch the spiral
tresses on the child's head.
She backs away, clambers
onto daddy's lap, thrusts her fingers
underneath his baseball cap,
where after months of fallowness,
shoots of yellow now protrude.

Her father chants behind the paper
mask that holds the germs at bay:
Fuzzy Wuzzy was a bear,
Fuzzy Wuzzy had no hair.
Fuzzy Wuzzy wasn't fuzzy, was he?
The child's giggle ricochets,
a bullet of jocundity
that slays the room's solemnity.

Clipboard underneath her arm,
a smiling woman smocked in blue
bellows out the father's name.
She pats his shoulder, jokes about
deserting her for half a year,
asks about his saxophone,
marvels at his daughter's growth.

Distracted by a patch of light,
the child scrambles to the floor,
where toys of every shape and shade
are strewn about like autumn leaves.
She opens up her mother's purse,
becomes immersed in keys and pens,
and doesn't seem to notice
when her father's wheeled away.

A VISIT TO THE HEALER

The stricken
pack the altar's grate,
waiting for the red-robed sage
to turn affliction into ash.

Stoked by their consuming need,
he flares and glows with holiness,
chanting as he lays his thumb
on foreheads blistering with hope.

Watching bodies drop like logs,
I long to blaze with true belief
but only smolder, spark-less,
on the chilly hearth of intellect.

NOCTURNAL RITUAL

At two in the morning, and three, and four,
he cuts my sleep with the shears of his need,
blunted for months from overuse.

I stumble around the double bed
and lift the legs the drugs have rendered
limp as post-alarm clock dreams.

I lower him into the wheelchair,
steer him into night-light gauze,
guide him onto the railing'd seat

and wait for his flush,
counting the hours before I must waken
the children for school.

He stands, then tumbles,
a tree devoid of resistance to insects
that feed on its innards.

His thanks and apologies
furrow the rug as I wheel him back,
and once again, we say good-night.

I throw myself at repose's feet,
unable to answer his whispered *Why
should I keep up the fight?*

THE HARDEST QUESTION

Moon-faced from the pills you take
to quell the swelling in your brain,
you gaze at me with eyes that once
were hazel suns—
now black holes where gravity
allows no light to come or go.

You want to know what day it is,
if lunch is soon, if it has snowed.
I grip my patience by the wrist
as if it were a two-year-old
about to vanish in a crowd
and answer you as if you hadn't
asked already, many times.

You muse about a childhood friend,
a paper cut, a T.V. show,
then blurt the question lurking
in your chatter like humidity:

Am I dying?

Past promises of honesty
coil around me like a boa,
choking out a skinny *Yes*
that slithers in and out of your head,

devouring calm, laying no eggs.

JEANS

No longer able
to stand alone,
he sits on the edge
of the unmade bed,
eyeing the denim enemy
I've laid upon his lap.

His fingers grip
the waistband
with desire
and determinedness
that interlock
like zipper teeth.
Bending slowly
toward his toes,
he tries to slide
the trousers
over flaccid feet,
wobbling like a tired top.

He flushes
like a schoolboy
who cannot recite
his ABCs,
straightens up and curses,
repeats the scene
with no success.
I feel goose bumps
on my flesh
as sweat runs down
his brow and neck.

A wild urge
to intervene
races through
my every cell, bucking
as I lasso it
with visions
of his trampled face
when last I galloped
to his aid.

Bridling my need,
I wait.

HOSPICE

Is this where people go
to die?
you ask the nurse who wheels you
to a room still rattling with the breath
of one who left an hour before.
Some go home, the nurse replies.

You know she's lying.

*

I plaster photos on the walls:
our children dressed for Halloween,
your sister with her newborn son,
your parents on our wedding day,
our kitten playing with a ball.
The kids hang drawings they have made.

Dozing, you don't notice.

*

The doctor says that you can eat
what long has been forbidden you.
I bring a box of chocolates,
the kind you once could not resist.
You stare at the assorted shapes,
then turn away.

I eat them all myself.

*

A toddler in the family lounge
spies a leashed Dalmatian pup
capering down the corridor.

The child's squeals cacophanize
with periodic moaning
from the room across from yours.

The dog lets loose a howl.

*

A gown now drapes the hanger
that was once your muscled
arms and chest. Asleep between
the bars of your electric bed,
you tug the faded fabric
till you're naked as a newborn.

I hide your diaper with a sheet.

*

Puffing like a locomotive,
suddenly you bare your teeth,
as if you're trying to smile at Death
but don't know how. I rub
your bluing legs and feet,
assure you I will be okay.

A thrush on the window ledge flies away.

METAMORPHOSIS

This morning you lay
in your double-jointed
hospice bed,
thanking me repeatedly
for tiny kindnesses:
a sip of water, a pillow
propped behind your head,
a blanket draped across your feet.

You held my hand
against your tissue paper lips,
declaring that your love for me
would soon devour your disease.
But now you turn and face the wall,
as if the very sight of me
were apt to make your bedsores bleed.

I rub your back between the rails
that hold you in like corset stays
and offer tea, a bite of toast, a magazine.
You flail me with refusals,
request that you be left alone.

Hobbling to the family lounge,
I ask the hours why they fashioned
tinder from your tenderness,
too unnerved to realize

it's easier to slam the door
than tiptoe out with teary eyes.

THE ULTIMATE ACT

I do not want my life to be prolonged, nor do I want life-sustaining treatment to be provided or continued if my agent believes the burdens of the treatment outweigh the expected benefits.

Your scribbled initials kick their feet
in language dense as Dead Sea brine,
splashing me with promises
I made when you were rosy-cheeked.

I wander your eroded shore,
thinking of the plans you had
for when the skeleton of Time
began to grow a bit of flesh.

I ache for you to take those trips
to Tokyo and Timbuktu,
to learn to do some magic tricks,
to read Euripides in Greek.

But love must overpower dreams,
so, summoning the man in white,
I ask to disconnect the tubes
that feed you Being in saline.

VISIT NUMBER ONE

A flock of pansies roosts on the grave
where we planted you in early spring.

Their dainty wings flap gold and violet
into April's spotless green.

I walk across the grass and find
the stubby sign that marks you

like a pack of watermelon seeds
stapled on a wooden stick.

I wonder whether I should talk
to you who cannot hear my voice,

to tell you all the latest news
and share what it is like to be

a universe of loneliness.

A man beyond the road dividing
cross from star

lies down upon the strips of sod
that stripe a plot without a stone.

I want to hug his heaving trunk,
to tell him he is not alone.

Instead, I place a pebble
by your name to show that I was here.

Plodding past neglected graves
whose bones have long divorced their flesh,

I exit through the gate and see
a sign across the busy street:

"Salsa music nightly, live."

CLEAN SWEEP

Your pin stripes and plaids
dangle on branches of papered wire,
faded leaves awaiting my rake.

I watch them flap in the gusts of my grief
each time I retrieve a shirt or a suit
from the closet we shared some twenty years.

I shake them down, bag them in plastic,
call for a truck to haul them away,
unable to bear the memories

that smolder in their folds and seams—
only to find that barrenness
burns hotter than remembrance.

THE FALLOUT OF LOSS

Below my heart-light
hang our daughter and her beau,
a diptych framed in tenderness.

I contemplate their every hue,
awed at how they flow
into a whole more wondrous than its halves,

and long to know the joy that comes
from seeing this creation glow
behind a shield of glare-free glass.

But all that I can feel is green,
remembering how you and I
once made each other so complete,

before the tumor vandalized
the glorious gallery in your head,
slashing all the canvases,

smearing them with excrement,
then stealing them to decorate
the living room of history.

FIRSTS

I

This birthday card, designed to tickle
even the most sober soul, evokes a pain
its cartoon drawings can't suppress.

It sits upon my desk for days
and waits for me to sign the names
I've grouped together countless times,

appellations intertwined as bone and flesh
till cancer's fingers plucked one out
and chiseled it upon a stone.

Reaching for a pen, I try
to write three signatures beneath
the greeting that should be from four,

but can't do more
than seal the card, affix a stamp,
and send it blank.

II

The room's a cornucopia
of those who share each other's blood.
I call them to a table clad
in crescent rolls and cranberries,
sweet potatoes, chestnut dressing,
gravy in a gold tureen.

We praise the Lord for plenitude,
begin the feast but cannot eat,

bloated as balloons with thoughts
of you who can no longer carve
the bird, or break the wishbone
when we've picked it clean.

III

Our child fidgets in her chair,
waiting for the principal
to call her name in spangled tones.

I hold a camera to my eye,
feeling like a girl her age
who's thrilled to get her first real kiss,
yet knows it isn't what she'd hoped.

I snap the shutter as she struts
across the stage and takes her plaque,
beaming with the self-same smile
you'd have right now if you were here.

I clap and cheer with all my heart—
that loveseat anchored in my chest
where pride holds hands with hollowness.

WIDOW

Encased in skin
as thin as the jokes
of a has-been comedian,
she blues at the bottom
of life's cold bin

a human onion
wondering if
she's being punished
for a sin
she didn't commit
or if her luck
has merely lost
its pungency.

Overwrought
by fear of rot,
she cannot see
that from her head
grow shoots the hue
of emeralds.

TREASURE

APRIL

Behind the door of her dressing room,
the diva warms up with ascending scales,
vibrato in her every note.

On cue she flounces onto the stage, .
her pompadour festooned with blue,
her feet in shoes of shamrock green.

Between the drizzle of recitatives,
she pours out arias of gold,
prompting cloudbursts of applause.

She bows with grace. The curtain drops.
She smugly struts into the wings,
knowing there'll be rave reviews.

BEDROOM BARD

In the ink of heat
you write your poems
upon my flesh

free of counted stresses
and expected rhymes,
yet with a subtle

irregular rhythm
that ripples my blood
and vibrates my bones.

You know exactly
where to break
your lines and stanzas

where to punctuate, and when
to leave the commas
and periods out,

revising till you're satisfied
that every syllable
is right.

MY DAUGHTER BECOMES A *BAT MITZVAH*

Without success, I've struggled
in this citadel of ritual
to feel the kiss of the Deity
and dodge the slap of unbelief.

But as I watch this new adult
in skullcap and embroidered shawl
unroll the sacred Torah scroll
and chant the ancient phrases
that have kept the Jewish people whole,

a sanctity I've never known
invades me like the fragrance
of azaleas in the spring—

born of motherlove and pride,
my longed-for link with the divine.

FOURTH OF JULY

Waves adorn the sand with lace
the wind crocheted from strands of spray
as twilight roosts upon the lake,
resting its head on its indigo breast.

Children brandish sticks ablaze
with diamonds, rubies, emeralds
that blind the flies on cups of punch
and sizzle the mosquitoes' wings.

A Sousa march begins to blare
from makeshift speakers on the pier,
brassing conversation
with a smattering of stars and stripes.

Propelled by a dissolving tail,
a glowing sperm
swims toward the cratered
egg ascending overhead,

changes into pink champagne
that bubbles in a glass of black,
then turns into a dandelion
past its prime.

The scene repeats incessantly
with fiery booms, with oohs and ahhhs,
until the sky, exhausted, pleads
for just an hour or two of sleep.

Shaking off our blankets, we
tread lighter through the jabs and shoves,
discarded cans, and car exhaust
that frost our nation's birthday cake.

TUBA MAN

While the pedigreed of Julliard
warm up in their tuxes and long
black skirts, a mutt of a man
in a loose Salvation Army coat
lobs grenades of notes at the throng
trooping into the concert hall.

He huffs and puffs a punishment
of brass and steel,
the instrumental equivalent
of Job's afflictions,
dented and scratched as if it had tumbled
off the roof of his zealousness.

Repeating a theme from *Die Meistersinger*
(the only tune he seems to know)
he sporadically motions toward his feet,
where an empty case lies open
like a toothless mouth that hankers
for the savory taste of dollar bills.

Later, when the trash cans brim
with ticket stubs and program notes,
the tuba man plays Wagner
to the rhythm of the city's snores,
practicing for tomorrow's performance,
a virtuoso of the ignored.

ORANGE

It glows in the bowl
like a flame Prometheus
stole from the gods
and molded into
a molten globe.

I plunge
into tenacious skin,
peeling it
in a single piece
I toss triumphantly
into the trash.

Gloved in lace,
the flesh inside
is tart and sweet
as an adolescent.

Extricating
all the seeds,
I suck the juice
from every section,
forgetting about
the host of woes
that kept me up
the night before,

until the fruit
is nothing more
than a plateful
of cicada wings.

CHEMISTRY

It's one of those mysteries
life so often
serves on platters made of air,

like the enigma
of who made God
if He created everything.

We lie with a lover
who strokes the places
we hold most sacred

and pray to be saved
by a telephone call
or a child's bad dream.

Then we lie with one
whose every move
resembles the other's like rosary beads

and sprouting wings,
we fly
to the Divine's domain.

MELODY OF HOPE

Night towels down
this house of tears
and powders it
with soundlessness.
Brushed and gowned,
I lie in bed,
too grieved to dream,
too tired to toss,

picturing for the hundredth time
the box of pine
tucked neatly
in a pocket
of the earth's green skirt,

trying to make myself believe
that happiness
will once again
curl up with me
and warm the sheets
of memory.

It's then I hear
the singing
of my child
in the room next door,
she who'd gone to bed
for weeks
pajama'd in despondency.

Her voice is soft
as feline feet,
yet unmistakably serene.

I close my eyes and fall asleep.

SOMERSET PENNSYLVANIA, 2002

They were hard
as the earth
that consumed them
at sunrise
and spat them up
when the whistle blew

tobacco chewers
who pelted each other
with digs and ribs
and four-letter words
they'd slap their kids
for using

here-and-now'ers
who threw their feelings
down the shaft
and left them there
to fossilize
with those of their fathers
and grandfathers.

But when the mine
that paid their bills
and bought their beer
collapsed and filled
with neck-high water
frigid as the breath of Dread

they scrawled farewells
of tenderness
to children, wives, and friends above,
stuffed them
in a lunch pail hung
above the swell

and tied themselves together
to ensure that no one
died alone.

A CONCERT
AT THE RETIREMENT HOME

In a windowless room
papered in peeling
gaiety, the widows and widowers
watch the band from folding chairs.

A woman taps her walker to the music's
beat, always just a trace
too late; a man
as veined as a subway map
chatters to an empty seat, oblivious
to shushes that transform
sonority to slush. A lady
dressed in pearls and lace
snores like a drunk
in an alleyway; another in a wheelchair
yowls refrains
that cause her hearing aid to shriek.

                    *

Dressed in concert black and white,
the musicians on the makeshift stage
radiate like neon.

Their faces, lined and spotted
as the pages on their portable stands,
vibrate with elation
as they inundate the afternoon
with sound they didn't learn to make
until their hair had long turned gray.

Her cane tucked safely out of sight,
the clarinetist starts a phrase; the flutist
joins her joyfully, ignoring

the aches in her finger joints.
The saxophonist blows until
he gleams with sweat more copious
than that from last year's heart attack;
the drummer thrums with steadiness
he struggled to regain for months
following his latest stroke.

*

The score of aging contains no directions
for changes in tempo, dynamics, and key
to help the players make it
to the double bar triumphantly.

ICICLE

This dangling sword
formed from the tears
of days too short
to reach the sun
slices the eye
with bladed shimmer,

a phallus of winter
dripping its crystal
between the tentative
legs of noon,
siring shards that sparkle
as they slicken
unsuspecting soles.

So much like life,
this digit
of frigidity,
which dazzles
like the smile of God
while pointing the way
to Satan's cave.

SOLICITOR

August weeps upon her neck,
drenching a tank top wide as the state
she traipses in plastic flip-flops.

She rings my bell, takes three steps back,
and waves a laminated badge
to shoo away my coolness.

I listen to her sales pitch,
watch her twiddle beaded braids
as if they might bestow the luck of rabbits' feet.

Uneasiness beseeches me
to bid her leave and lock the door,
then gags upon

my growing admiration at her self-belief,
which swoops her through unwelcomeness
on steel wings.

I offer her some lemonade
and buy a year's subscription
to a magazine I'll never read.

AFTER E.E. CUMMINGS'S
PORTRAIT VIII

("Buffalo Bill's")

Ludwig van B's

decomposed

    who used to

        squeeze out genius like

                lemonade

and slake onetwothreefourfive parched souls   justlikethat

                        Freude notwithstanding

he was a troubled man

        and what I want to know is

how did you concoct such sweetness

Mister Deaf?

MR. KUZUMI'S EPIPHANY

Decades ago our round-eyed compatriots
bombed us with orders to vacate our homes
and settle in camps where essentials of living
were scanty as hair on a middle-aged man.

They saw us as clones of their foes, unaware
that our hearts, like theirs,
were starred and striped.

Their injustices rise in my memory's sky
like the sun on the flag of my grandparents' birth
as I sit in this interfaith vigil for victims
of terrorist ire on American soil

and listen to speeches that plead for support
for the enemy's look-alikes here in our midst,
citizens hoisting the red, white, and blue
on poles of outrage and boundless grief.

Singing "The Star Spangled Banner" with those
whose skins bleed together to form a new shade,
I realize history need not repeat.

ROLE MODEL

Each autumn,
the valleys
lavish the artist
with willow wands
he gathers and bundles,
handling them
as if they were
as fragile
as October's rays.

Planted on his studio floor,
he sorts his cache
by strength and size,
submerges the stalks
in dyes the shades
of Joseph's coat,
and lets them dry.

He starts to weave
without a scheme,
with only faith
to guide his hands,
which sometimes
break a reed in half
or choose two hues
that clash
like Hatfields and McCoys

but deftly use
the tool
of serendipity
required to make
a masterpiece.

BED FOR ONE

Late at night my singleness—
a jalapeño when it's light—
is luscious as a chocolate truffle.

I snuggle underneath the quilt
in baggy pajamas and mismatched socks,
a massive novel on my lap,
unobliged to muffle my lamp
or exhalations of my gut.

When sleep arrives, it always stays,
never chased away by snores
or shivers from a stolen quilt.

Next morning, when I wake with breath
malodorous as sewer gas,
I needn't rush to brush my teeth.

Kings and queens have always known
what others fail to comprehend:
preferring solitude in bed
has nothing to do with lust or love.

THE URBAN BIRDS

High above the workday streets,
where people scatter like billiard balls,
a flock of identical, speckled wings
swoops and sails in perfect sync,
as if its leader held a mighty
magnet in her beak. The creatures
rise and fall like waltzers
crowded into a ballroom of cloud,
displaying an uncanny knack
for knowing just exactly when
to change their path
from south to north or west to east,
while the city spins, unable to feel
the kiss of precision
on its cheek.

ABOUT THE AUTHOR

Susan Spaeth Cherry was a journalist for twenty years, writing for newspapers and magazines nationwide as both a staff member and a free-lancer. A persistent need to express herself creatively lead her to start writing poetry in mid-life. Her work, which has won many awards, has been published in literary magazines and poetry anthologies. She is the author of two poetry collections: *Hole to Whole* and *Sonata in the Key of Being.* Two of her poems have been set to music.

A resident of suburban Chicago, Cherry has done many local poetry readings and has taught workshops at area schools, as well as at Harvard College. She has been a member of the selective Poets' Club of Chicago for many years. Cherry is the mother of two daughters, who often inspire her work.